I Never Travel Without My Diary. One Should Always Have Something Sensational To Read On The Train.

- O. Wilde -

This book belongs to:

....

....

Printed by Amazon Italia Logistica S.r.l.
Torrazza Piemonte (TO), Italy

59831898R00065